Up, Up and Away!

ISBN 978-1-0980-4828-0 (paperback)
ISBN 978-1-0980-4829-7 (hardcover)
ISBN 978-1-0980-4830-3 (digital)

Christian Faith Publishing, Inc.
832 Park Avenue
Meadville, PA 16335
www.christianfaithpublishing.com

Printed in the United States of America

CPSIA information can be obtained
at www.ICGtesting.com
Printed in the USA
BVHW020502061220
595017BV00001B/4

Up, Up
and Away!

A Children's Book
on Revelation

Dorothy Skiles

Illustrated by Gordon Rumble

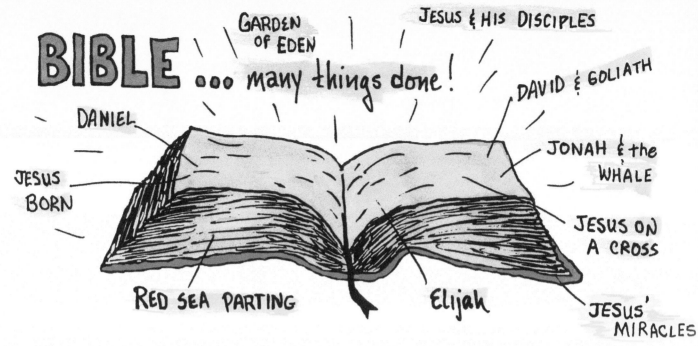

BIBLE ... many things done!

GARDEN OF EDEN

JESUS & HIS DISCIPLES

DAVID & GOLIATH

DANIEL

JONAH & the WHALE

JESUS BORN

JESUS ON A CROSS

RED SEA PARTING

Elijah

JESUS' MIRACLES

"Do you believe the BIBLE is GOD'S WORD?"

This story is real from the Bible, you see.
It is prophetic, which means, "Yet to be."

God in His Word tells of things that are done,
things that are now and things that will come.

Revelation 1:1–3

BIBLE .... many things "YET TO BE!"

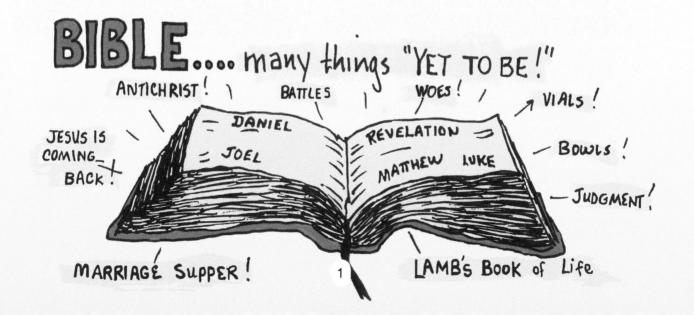

ANTICHRIST!

BATTLES

WOES!

VIALS!

JESUS IS COMING BACK!

DANIEL

JOEL

REVELATION

MATTHEW   LUKE

BOWLS!

JUDGMENT!

MARRIAGE SUPPER!

LAMB'S BOOK of Life

My name is John. My job was to fish, then Jesus called my name.
I became a disciple, a fisher of men, and lived His fame to proclaim.

I wrote the book of Revelation as God inspired me.
It's His plan for the future. Keep on reading, and you'll see.

Mark 1:16–20

Since the Garden of Eden, every heart is born with sin.
But God promised a Savior to redeem the souls of men.

Jesus Christ is the Messiah, the King we've waited so long for.
Now He is ascended up to heaven, but wait there is so much more!

Acts 1:9-11
Romans 3:23
Romans 5:6-10

The Lord told all His followers to share with others and to teach,
of His love and His forgiveness and His saving grace—Go preach!

Because I taught that Jesus is Lord, "He is God," I did exclaim,
I was captured and placed on an island—Isle of Patmos is its name.

Matthew 28:18–20
Revelation 1:9–10

4

Suddenly a loud voice caused me to look up in fright.
It happened quick and was scary, but oh what a sight!

Jesus was speaking, His eyes fiery bright,
wearing a sash and a sword with hair snowy white.

Revelation 1:9–16

Then He said, "I am First, I am Last, I am Jesus, you know,
of things in the future to you I will show.

It's called Revelation, so take a good look.
I want you to watch this and then write a book."

Revelation 1:17-19

As God revealed the vision right before my very eyes,
I wrote it down so in the future there would be no great surprise.

I sent letters to seven churches to remind them of God's ways,
to keep Him first, to love Him more, and serve Him all their days.

Revelation 2 and 3

God's promise to His children is to take us all away
before the punishment of sin on that dreadful
judgment day.

This punishment is for the ones who have been told and know,
of God's saving grace, yet in their hearts, they still
reply, "No, no!"

Romans 1:18–27
Romans 6:23

"Be ready," "Stay alert," He's coming back. The time is near.
Rapture is the word we use when Jesus says, "Come up here!"

Jesus keeps His promises and will return one day,
to catch all who believe in Him, into the clouds—
Up, up and away!

Matthew 24:36, 42, 44
1 Thessalonians 4:13–18
Revelation 4:1–2

"7 YEARS"

Seven years of Tribulation, God lets Satan be the one
to bring trouble and destruction until this time is done.

Satan has his men to do his plan. They are really, really mean.
The antichrist and false prophet, the most evil men you've seen.

Matthew 24:4-28
2 Thessalonians 2:3-4
Revelation 13

"Sure Sounds Scary"

"false prophet in sheep's clothing"

"Judgment Coming!"

God pours out righteous judgment on earth and on man.
It's really quite scary, but all part of His plan,

To show us His power over Satan and sin,
for man to repent and accept Jesus within.

Daniel 9:24–27
2 Peter 3:7, 9
1 John 3:8

Seals, trumpets, and bowls full of horrible things
Will pour out destruction on man and will bring...

Hunger, fire, hail, locusts, the rivers run dry, earthquakes, boils and darkness, all people will cry!

Revelation 6, 8, 9, 16

And then there's Armageddon, the worst battle of all time.
Satan gives one last effort to control all mankind.

His goal has always been even now and in the past
to wipe out God's chosen people and be done with
them at last.

Revelation 19:11-21

But as always, God's in charge and sends His Son again
with an army of the raptured saints who have a great
big win!

One thousand years, the Millennium, when Satan's bound up tight,
we'll live in peace, Jesus will reign, and everything will be made right!

Revelation 20:1–6

DEVIL
CHAINED

The Great White Throne Judgment is for those who don't believe in the saving grace of Jesus and their punishment receive.

Satan and all evil men will stand before God face-to-face.
He sends them to their final home—hell, darkness, and pain, what an awful place!

Revelation 20:11–15

"Lamb's Book of Life"

"Is your name in this book?"

But there is Good News once Satan is bound,
in the Lamb's Book of Life all names will be found.

Names of the redeemed, those saved and restored,
who are cleansed by the blood of Jesus their Lord.

Daniel 12:1
Ephesians 1:7
Revelation 3:5
Revelation 20:12, 15
Revelation 21:27

"Welcome Home!"

"ETERNITY! THAT'S A LONG TIME!"

Life forever is started; it isn't the end.
It's victory! It's beautiful! Let eternity begin!

But what's heaven like? Jesus in person for real!
He's the center, the focus! He is the big deal!

John 3:16
1 Corinthians 15:51-57
Revelation 1:1-8

God has made a new heaven and earth. It is grand!
Streets of gold, gates of pearl, a special feast has been planned.

The Marriage Supper of the Lamb with yummy food galore.
Pizza, popcorn, ice cream, cake, candy, hot dogs—
Have some more!

Revelation 19:9
Revelation 21:1, 21

Heaven is a celebration! Great rejoicing as we meet,
David, Noah, Jonah, all our friends, worshipping at Jesus's feet.

In the twinkling of an eye our whole life will be made new.
We'll be given perfect bodies, brand new clothes, a
mansion too!

John 14:1–3
1 Corinthians 15:42–44, 52
1 John 3:2
Revelation 4:4, 10, 11

There is no sun in heaven because Jesus is the light.
It is forever daytime, no more sleeping, no more night.

Heaven is magnificent; there is nothing like it here.
The tree of life, the throne of God and rivers running
crystal clear.

Isaiah 60:19, 20
Revelation 21:23–25
Revelation 22:1–5

"I will not need my flashlight anymore!"

No chores, no naps, and no beds to make.
No cuts, no bruises, and no more baths to take.

No crying, no pain, God will wipe every tear.
Satan has been defeated; there is nothing to fear.

Revelation 21:4

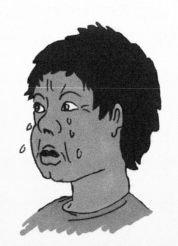

Angels and saints are praising and singing,
trumpets, harps, and voices all loudly are ringing.

Hallelujah! God reigns! Worship Jesus the Lamb!
King of kings! Lord of lords! He is the Great I AM!

Revelation 4:8
Revelation 5:9-14
Revelation 15:3-4

22

It's awesome! It's wonderful! You don't want to miss out!
Accept Jesus as your Savior, then you'll hear Him shout.

To call all His children to heaven someday. Keep looking and watching for that glorious day!

Luke 21:27, 28
John 3:16-17
John 6:40

"Come up,

up and

away!"

1 Thessalonians 4:13–18
Revelation 4:1

24

About the Author

Dorothy Skiles was raised in a Christian home and feels privileged to have been called by the Lord to be His child. She and her husband, Dale, have been blessed with three children and six grandchildren. After studying the end-times, Dorothy became inspired to present the book of Revelation and the return of Jesus to her grandchildren in the form of a children's book. Ultimately, her passion is to encourage others to desire the Word of God, draw closer to Jesus, and love the Lord in a deeper way.

About the Illustrator

Gordon Rumble is a pastor at Big Valley Grace Community Church. He is married to Heidi, and together they have three children and nine grandchildren. His excitement and teaching of eschatology have been an inspiration to many. Gordon has written the book *Revelation, Lessons from the Last Lap Home*, which is a commentary on the end-times. He has been a pastor for forty years and enjoys using his God-given talent of drawing for the Lord's work.